How To Start Your Own Coffee Business

Your Business Plan, Wholesale Supplies, Coffee Shop Book

By

Colwell Bowen

Table of Contents

Chapter 1..9
    Coffee Shop Business Overview......................9
Chapter 2..17
    Coffee Shop Equipment & Supplies..............17
Chapter 3..37
    Best Way To Write A Business Plan...............37
Chapter 4..45
    Crowd Funding...45
Chapter 5..51
    $5 Million Dollars to Fund Your Business 51
Chapter 6..57
    Marketing How To Reach a Billion People for Free! 57
Chapter 7..71
    Business Insurance...71
Chapter 8..79
    Business Terms..79

ABOUT THE AUTHOR

Brian Mahoney is the author of over 463 business start-up books, real estate investing programs and Christian literature. He started his company MahoneyProducts in 1992.

He served 2 tours in the US Army, worked for Walt Disney World and worked over a decade for the US Postal Service. He currently runs multiple online businesses and has also served as a minister for the Churches of Christ in Virginia and Michigan.

He has degree's in Business Administration and Applied Science & Computer Programming.

His books and video training programs have helped thousands of people all over the world start there own successful business.

http://www.briansmahoney.com/

Disclaimer

This book was written as a guide to starting a business. As with any other high yielding action, starting a business has a certain degree of risk. This book is not meant to take the place of accounting, legal, financial or other professional advice. If advice is needed in any of these fields, you are advised to seek the services of a professional.

While the author has attempted to make the information in this book as accurate as possible, no guarantee is given as to the accuracy or currency of any individual item. Laws and procedures related to business are constantly changing.

Therefore, in no event shall Brian Mahoney, the author of this book be liable for any special, indirect, or consequential damages or any damages whatsoever in connection with the use of the information herein provided.

All Rights Reserved

No part of this book may be used or reproduced in any manner whatsoever without the written permission of the author.

Join Our VIP Mailing List and Get FREE Money Making Training Videos! Then Start Making Money within 24 hours!
Plus if you join our Mailing list you can get Revised and New Edition versions of your book free!

And Notifications of other FREE Offers!

Just Hit/Type in the Link Below

https://mahoneyproducts.wixsite.com/win1

Copyright © 2019 Brian Mahoney
All rights reserved.

Chapter 1

Coffee Shop Business Overview

COFFEE SHOP BUSINESS OVERVIEW

Start-cost: $25,000 - $45,000

Potential earnings: $5,000 - $20,000 per month

Typical fees: $2,50 - $5.00 per cup

Advertisig: Social Media, Flyers and Commercials.

Qualifications: Retail & Restaurant experience related to purchasing, marketing and customer service. The ability to prepare coffee, tea and other products.

Equipment needs: Coffee/tea brewing equipment. Cups, food, refrigerators, cooking, furniture, cash register and other equipment.

Home business: No

Staff required: Yes

Hidden costs: Zoning and local business license fees. Location casts and business insurance.

COFFEE SHOP BUSINESS OVERVIEW

A coffee shop, also known as a cafe' or coffeehouse is a business whose main product is coffee, but sells other coffee drinks like espresso, cappuccino and latte. More and more coffee shops are serving cold drinks like iced tea and energy beverages. Coffee shops in the United States also serve pastries, muffins, light snacks, fruit and sandwiches.

Coffee is second only to water as the most popular drink on the planet. Coffee is billion dollar industry and a small coffee shop can make $5,000 to $20,000 a month.

Having a successful coffee shop business as with any business, begins with good planning. You must write a good business plan and begin with the end in mind. Knowing your ultimate goal. Do you just want to own one coffee shop business or do you plan on francising? A good business plan is also necessary for you to get loans from financial institutions.

Later in this book I will cover how to write a business plan in detail. Later in the coffee shop equipment and supplies chapter I included the price ranges of most of the equipment to help you estimate the start up cost of your coffee shop business which will be important when looking for a business startup loans from the government.

COFFEE SHOP BUSINESS OVERVIEW

Location. You must choose a high traffic location that is properly zoned for your business. You will either need to rent space or purchase a location. Read your lease. Don't be afraid to negotiate. Negotiate the rent, and ask for free months to help you get started Alls a landlord can do is say no. So shop around for your location.

Have exclusive agreements like forbiding other tenants from selling coffee as long as your business is there leasing. Also, no other new tenants will be allowed to sell coffee beans or brewed coffee, tea, smoothies and any product your business depends on.

Option to Sublet Property. Most leases allow you to do this, but make sure you have it in your lease. You might want to leave before the lease is up and you want to be sure you can sublet the property for the remainder of the lease.

Branding. Your shop should stand out form other coffee shops. Green is Starbucks, Orange is Biggby. Both have accommodations for comfortable stays. Biggby has Television sets and Starbucks has free wifi. What will make your shop stand out?

COFFEE SHOP BUSINESS OVERVIEW

While you want your shop to have it's own brand, don't try to reinvent the wheel. Take advantage of all the market research that big successful franchises have done. Things like free wifi, menu ideas, and pricing.

Having worked for the Walt Disney Corporation, I can not stress the importance of customer service. People have plenty of options, and if they perceive that they are not being treated professionally they will go somewhere else. Try to hire mature people and help them to understand that their income comes from the people who patronize your business.

Set up a business bank account. You may pay more in service fees than you would for a personal account. However, a credit union account will save money in fees even for a business.

Shop around for your business financing. You have banks, credit unions, Small Business Administration government loans and crowdfunding.

COFFEE SHOP BUSINESS OVERVIEW

Obtain the necessary business licenses and permits. If you are not sure check with the local municipality about zoning ordinances. You don't want to sign a lease for space and then later discover, that you can' operate your business the way you want to because of restrictions you were not aware of.

If you are not good with accounting, then hire an accountant that will help you to maximize your business tax deductions.

Decide what type of business you are going to have. A corporation, partnership or sole proprietor. There are advantages and disadvantages to all.

Talk to a independent insurance broker and have this broker shop around for the best busness insurance. Later in this book there is an entire chapter on business insurance.

COFFEE SHOP BUSINESS OVERVIEW

Even if you are located in a high traffic area, you need to do marketing. It could be as simple as having business cards at the cash register and have a professional looking web site. In todays world of the disappearing newspaper, the marketing of choice is "permission marketing" (building an email customer list). In marketing it helps to know search engine optimization or SEO. SEO relates to other forms of marketing such as Google Ads and YouTube Videos. I will cover marketing in more detail later in this book.

Finally expect hard work. Read or view biographies on the greatest most successful business people and you will see they overcame tremendous obstacles. Walt Disney had mutiple bankruptcies. Warren Buffet had to survive government inquiries. Marvel Studios went bankrupt and had to sell the rights to many of their properties.

You have a vision. Not everbody will share that vision or have your desire, energy and enthusiasm. Don't be afraid to make "half time adjustments". In other words see what works and does not work and let your business evolve and grow, and trim any weeds that may be choking out your success.

Chapter 2

Coffee Shop Equipment & Supplies

Coffee Shop Equipment

Coffee Shop equipment comprehensive list of supplies.

Web Site links sometimes change, so I have given you a web link directly to the product. However, just in cast the link changes, I have included the website home page.

1. Blender

https://www.coffeeam.com/

https://goo.gl/mQpR9A

($298 - $3,105)

2. Brewer: coffee

https://www.coffeeam.com/

https://goo.gl/ymaqnd

($265 - $3,097)

Coffee Shop Equipment

3. Brewer: tea

https://www.coffeeam.com/

https://goo.gl/xebqXr

($663 - $891)

4. Coffee grinder

https://www.coffeeam.com/

https://goo.gl/tL1WxR

($445 - $4,595)

5. Cash register

https://www.webstaurantstore.com

https://goo.gl/EhFfgg

($259 - $399)

Coffee Shop Equipment

6. Coffee maker

https://www.appliancesconnection.com/

https://goo.gl/FYbDX8

($29 - $602)

7. Credit card machine

www.nationalbankcard.com

https://goo.gl/6qy618

($125 - $250)

8. Decanters airpots satellite servers

https://www.coffeeam.com/

https://goo.gl/8pc1nq

($7.95 - $79.97)

Coffee Shop Equipment

9. Espresso grinders

https://www.webstaurantstore.com

https://goo.gl/cmKwBy

($688 - $1,274)

10. Espresso machine

https://www.coffeeam.com/

https://goo.gl/f2uben

($1,995 - $21,200)

11. Freezer

https://www.appliancesconnection.com/

https://goo.gl/8yikSQ

($217 - $2,249)

Coffee Shop Equipment

12. Food supplies

https://www.coffeeam.com

Coffee

https://www.coffeeam.com/gourmet-coffee.html

($11.95 - $59.95)

Tea

https://www.coffeeam.com/gourmet-tea.html

($4.95 - $89.95)

Pastry

https://www.danishpastryhouse.com/wholesale-pastry/

Coffee Shop Equipment

Variety of food/snacks

https://www.foodservicedirect.com/foods.html

13. Furniture

https://www.restaurantfurniture4less.com/

https://goo.gl/PJ7yFf

($8.99 - $3,484)

14. Hot water dispenser

https://www.coffeeam.com/

https://goo.gl/u7NY5Q

($89.95 - $1,491)

15. Ice maker

https://www.appliancesconnection.com/

https://goo.gl/QGtNjd

($149-$4,400)

Coffee Shop Equipment

16. Oven

https://www.appliancesconnection.com/

https://goo.gl/e5zGWv

($894 - $23,059)

17. Panini grill

https://www.Walmart.com

https://goo.gl/2QbCS8

($29.99-$39.99)

18. Pastry case refrigerated

https://www.webstaurantstore.com/

https://goo.gl/nwE7GH

($1,799 - $2,400)

Coffee Shop Equipment

19. Pastry case not refrigerated

https://www.webstaurantstore.com/

https://goo.gl/jjntNM

($69-$387)

20. Phone

https://www.walmart.com/

https://goo.gl/kNuvZc

($14.97 - $1,099)

21. Radio system

https://www.markertek.com/

https://goo.gl/RN3hE6

($534)

Coffee Shop Equipment

22. Refrigerator under counter

https://www.appliancesconnection.com/

https://goo.gl/tktU6w

($159 - $3,857)

23. Refrigerator storage

https://www.appliancesconnection.com/

https://goo.gl/b3gtPN

($1,192 - $9,430)

24. Sandwich prep unit

https://www.appliancesconnection.com/

https://goo.gl/xS3Mys

($1,693 - $4,025)

Coffee Shop Equipment

25. Sink

https://www.webstaurantstore.com/

https://goo.gl/3CguCB

($162 - $2,117)

26. Tea dispenser

https://www.webstaurantstore.com/

https://goo.gl/eAyp3h

($55.99 - $153.99)

27. Dishwasher

https://www.webstaurantstore.com

https://goo.gl/Wk6p43

($2,589 - $7,174)

Coffee Shop Equipment

28. Espresso tampers

https://www.wholelattelove.com/

https://goo.gl/bTGLsP

($5.90 - $124.99)

29. Frothing pitchers

https://www.webstaurantstore.com

https://goo.gl/UbGD3K

($3.50 - $11.50)

30. Knock boxes

https://www.espressoparts.com/

https://goo.gl/qfiamL

https://www.baristaproshop.com/

https://goo.gl/SDAK6w

($31.00 - $104.95)

Coffee Shop Equipment

31. Measuring cups and spoons

https://www.webstaurantstore.com/

https://goo.gl/fGiiJL

($0.64 - $38.99)

32. Scales

https://www.webstaurantstore.com/

https://goo.gl/SDwmEU

($18.70 - $1,560)

33. Security system

ADT

https://goo.gl/cRXmVv

SimpliSafe

https://simplisafe.com/business-security

Coffee Shop Equipment

34. Syrup pumps

https://www.coffeeam.com/

https://goo.gl/zGi9x3

($3.95 - $79.95)

35. Frothing thermometers

https://www.webstaurantstore.com/

https://goo.gl/Jhf9HW

($2.34 - $6.16)

36. Timers

https://www.webstaurantstore.com/

https://goo.gl/eP7wC1

($3.09 - $789.80)

Coffee Shop Equipment

37. Coffee mugs and tea cups

https://www.discountmugs.com/

https://goo.gl/9Z9Vgw

($0.61 - $44.34)

38. Espresso cup

https://www.discountmugs.com/

https://goo.gl/viBKjD

($1.17 - $8.87)

39. Dinnerware

https://www.webstaurantstore.com/

https://goo.gl/Tc8vsw

https://www.coffeeshopsolutions.com/

https://goo.gl/6Zu6iv

Coffee Shop Equipment

40. Tea ball infusers lemon wedge bags

https://www.walmart.com

https://goo.gl/XTHTSV

https://goo.gl/tCaMMR

($1.22 - $19.99)

Lemon wedge bags

https://www.walmart.com

https://goo.gl/rSgwwu

41. Sugar pourers

https://www.webstaurantstore.com/

https://goo.gl/wJda1M

($1.05 - $1.63)

Coffee Shop Equipment

42. Creamers

https://www.webstaurantstore.com/

https://goo.gl/NdfMcV

($1.29 - $30.18)

43. Condiment organizers

https://www.webstaurantstore.com/

https://goo.gl/Wq7WoY

($2.17 - $48.99)

44. cup, lid, and straw organizers

https://www.hotcupfactory.com/

https://www.hotcupfactory.com/c-64-hot-paper-cups.aspx

($14.64 - $84.64)

Coffee Shop Equipment

45. coffee and beverage labeling

https://www.stickermule.com/

https://goo.gl/DR92Uy

($55 - $846)

46. Aprons

https://www.walmart.com

https://goo.gl/fYXyTp

($3.57 - $34.99)

47. LED signs

https://www.webstaurantstore.com/

https://goo.gl/BN2S8L

($6.96 - $482.99)

Coffee Shop Equipment

48. Retail merchandisers

https://www.webstaurantstore.com/

https://goo.gl/kfdn7h

($19.99 - $156.99)

49. Replacement Parts

https://www.baristaproshop.com/

https://goo.gl/XszPiV

($4.75 - $35.65)

50. Warming Plates

https://www.coffeeam.com/

https://goo.gl/VPr21m

($37.95 - $159.95)

Chapter 3

Best Way To Write A Business Plan

How to Write a Business Plan

Millions of people want to know what is the secret to making money. Most have come to the conclusion that it is to start a business. So how to start a business? The first thing you do to start is business is to create a business plan.

A business plan is a formal statement of a set of business goals, the reasons they are believed attainable, and the plan for reaching those goals. It may also contain background information about the organization or team attempting to reach those goals.

A professional business plan consists of eight parts.

1. Executive Summary

The executive summary is a very important part of your business plan. Many consider it the most important because it this part of your plan gives a summary of the current state of your business, where you want to take it and why the business plan you have made will be a success. When requesting funds to start your business, the executive summary is an chance to get the attention of a possible investor.

How to Write a Business Plan

2. Company Description

The company description part of your business plan gives a high level review of the different aspects of your business. This is like putting your elevator pitch into a brief summary that can help readers and possible investors quickly grasp the goal of your business and what will make it stand out, or what unique need it will fill.

3. Market Analysis

The market analysis part of your business plan should go into detail about your industries market and monetary potential. You should demonstrate detailed research with logical strategies for market penetration. Will you use low prices or high quality to penetrate the market?

4. Organization and Management

The Organization and Management section follows the Market Analysis. This part of the business plan will have your companies organizational structure, the type of business structure of incorporation, the ownership, management team and the qualifications of everyone holding these positions including the board of directors if necessary.

How to Write a Business Plan

5. Service or Product Line

The Service or Product Line part of your business plan gives you a chance to describe your service or product. Focus on the benefits to the customers more than what the product or service does. For example, a air conditioner makes cold air. The benefit of the product is it cools down and makes customers more comfortable whether they are driving in bumper to bumper traffic or a sick and sitting in a nursing home. Air Conditioners fill a need that could mean the difference between life and death. Use this section to state what are the most important benefits of your product or service and what need it fills.

6. Marketing and Sales

Having a proven marketing plan is essential element to the success of any business. Today online sales are dominating the marketplace. Present a strong internet marketing plan as well as social media plan. YouTube videos, Facebook Ads and Press Releases all can be part of your internet marketing plan. Passing out flyers and business cards are still an effective way to reach potential customers.

Use this part of your business plan to state your projected sales and how you came to that number. Do your research on similar companies for possible statistics on sales numbers.

How to Write a Business Plan

7. Funding Request

When you write your Funding Request section of your business plan, be sure to be detailed and have documentation of the cost of supplies, building space, transportation, overhead and promotion of your business.

8. Financial Projections

The following is a list of the important financial statements to include in your business plan packet.

Historical Financial Data

Your historical financial data would be bank statements, balance sheets and possible collateral for your loan.

Prospective Financial Data

The prospective financial data section of your business plan should show you potential growth within your industry, projecting out for at least the next five years.

You can have monthly or quarterly projections for the first year. Then project from year to year.

Include a ratio and trend analysis for all of your financial statements. Use colorful graphs to explain positive trends, as part of the financial projections section of your business plan.

How to Write a Business Plan

Appendix

The appendix should not be part of the main body of your business plan. It should only be provided on a need to know basis. Your business plan may be seen by a lot of people and you don't want certain information available to everybody. Lenders may need such information so you should have an appendix ready just in case.

The appendix would include:

Credit history (personal & business)

- Resumes of key managers
- Product pictures
- Letters of reference
- Details of market studies
- Relevant magazine articles or book references
- Licenses, permits or patents
- Legal documents
- Copies of leases

How to Write a Business Plan

Building permits

Contracts

List of business consultants, including attorney and accountant

Keep a record of who you allow to see your business plan.

Include a Private Placement Disclaimer. A Private Placement Disclaimers is a private placement memorandum (PPM) is a document focused mainly on the possible downsides of an investment.

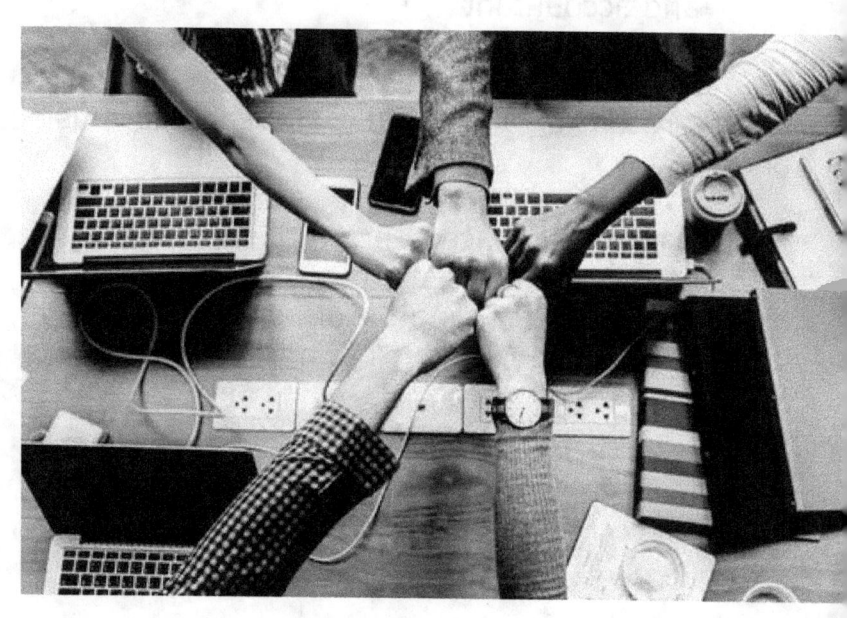

Chapter 4

Get Colossal Cash Free!
Crowd Funding

Crowd Funding Crowd Sourcing

In 2015 over $34 billion dollars was raised by crowdfunding. Crowdfunding and Crowdsourcing roots began in 2005 and they help to finance or fund projects by raising money from a large number of people, usually by using the internet.

This type of fundraising or venture capital usually has 3 components. The individual or organization with a project that needs funding, groups of people who donate to the project, and a organization sets up a structure or rules to put the tow together.

These websites do charge fees. The standard fee for success is about %5. If your goal is not met there is also a fee.

Below is a list of the top Crowdfunding websites according to myself and Entrepreneur Magazine Contributor Sally Outlaw.

Crowd Funding Crowd Sourcing

https://www.indiegogo.com/

Started as a platform for getting movies made, now helps to raise funds any cause.

http://rockethub.com/

Started as a platform for the arts, now it helps to raise funds for business, science, social projects and education.

http://peerbackers.com/

Peerbackers focuses on raising funds for business, entrepreneurs and innovators.

https://www.kickstarter.com/

The most popular and well know n of all the crowdfunding websites. Kickstarter focuses on film, music, technology, gaming, design and the creative arts. Kickstarter only accepts projects from the United States, Canada and the United Kingdom.

Crowd Funding Crowd Sourcing

http://group.growvc.com/

This website is for business and technology innovation.

https://microventures.com/

Get access to angel investors. This website is for business startups.

https://angel.co/

Another website for business startups.

https://circleup.com/

Circle up is for innovative consumer companies.

https://www.patreon.com/

If you start a YouTube Channel (highly recommended) you will hear about this website frequently. This website if for creative content people.

Crowd Funding Crowd Sourcing

https://www.crowdrise.com/

"Raise money for any cause that inspires you." Landing page slogan speaks for itself. #1 fundraising website for personal causes.

https://www.gofundme.com/

This fundraising website allows for business, charity, educatiion, emergencies, sports, medical, memorials, animals, faith, family, newlyweds etc...

https://www.youcaring.com/

The leader in free fundraising. Over $400 million raised.

https://fundrazr.com/

"FundRazr is laser-focused on eliminating the guesswork of raising money online for your campaign. Our technology and social media guidance make telling your powerful story easy; sharing it with the widest community simple; and collecting the money worry-free. "

Chapter 5

$5 Million Dollars to Fund Your Business

$5 Million Dollars to Fund Your Business

Loans guaranteed by the Small Business Administration can be as little as $500 to as big as $5 Million Dollars!

The money can be used for a variety of business needs, including the purchase of long-term fixed assets and for operating expenses. Some loan programs do have restrictions on how the loan money can be used, so you will have to check with a Small Business Administration approved lender when looking for a loan. The lender can match you with the correct loan for your business needs.

Working Capital

Like seasonal financing, export loans, revolving credit, and refinanced business debt.

Fixed Assets

Like office equipment, property, tools, machinery, business equipment, construction, and remodeling.

$5 Million Dollars to Fund Your Business

Eligibility requirements

Lenders and loan programs have distinctive eligibility guide lines. Basically, eligibility is related to what a business does to receive its funding, the character of its ownership, and location of the businesses operation. Usually, businesses must meet size standards.

What is a small business size standard?

A size standard, under most circumstances is stated in number of employees or average yearly receipts, and represents the biggest size that a business (including its subsidiaries and affiliates) may be to remain classified as a small business for Small Business Administration and government contracting programs. The definition of "small" can be different in different industries.

How to calculate your small business size

Size standards are mostly based on the average annual receipts or the average number of employees.

$5 Million Dollars to Fund Your Business

Eligibility requirements

You must be able to repay the loan. You must have a credible business objective. Individuals with bad credit may still qualify for business startup money. Lenders will give you a list of the lending guide lines and requirements for your loan. Here are a few more.

Be a for-profit business

The business is properly registered and performs as a legal business.

Do business in the U.S.

The business is physically located and operates in the United States and or its territories.

You Have invested equity

You the business owner has invested your own time or finances into the business.

$5 Million Dollars to Fund Your Business

Eligibility requirements

Exhaust financing options

The business cannot get money from any other financial lender.

Loans for exporters

Most United States banks view loans for exporters as risky. This can make it more difficult for you to get loans for things like day-to-day operations, advance orders with suppliers, and debt refinancing. That's why the Small Business Administration came up with programs to make it easier for United States small businesses to get loans for an export business.

To learn how the SBA can help you get an export loan, contact your local Small Business Administration International Trade Finance Specialist or the Small Business Administration's Office of International Trade.

https://www.sba.gov/funding-programs/loans

Chapter 6

Marketing How To Reach a Billion People for Free!

How to Reach a Billion People for Free!

Marketing your coffee shop business is essential to it's success. In today's business environment marketing does not have to be expensive. With social media and big search engines like Google and YouTube you can get your business in front of millions of people without it costing a fortune.

ZERO COST MARKETING

While there are many ways to market we are only going focus on ZERO COST MARKETING. You are starting up. You can always go for the more expensive ways of marketing after your business is producing income.

FREE WEB HOSTING

Get a free web site. You can get a free web site at weebly.com or wix.com. Or just type "free web hosting" in a google, bing or yahoo search engine.

Free web hosting is something you can use for a varietey or reasons. However many free web hosting sites add an extention to the name of you web address that lets everyone know you are using their services. For this reason you eventually want to scale up once you start making income.

How to Reach a Billion People for Free!

LOW COST PAID WEB HOSTING

Free is nice, but you when you need to expand your business it is best to go with a paid web hosting service. There are several that give you good value for under $10.00 a month.

1. Yahoo small business
2. Intuit.com
3. ipage.com
4. Hostgator.com
5. Godaddy.com

Yahoo small business allows for unlimited web pages and is probably the best overall value, but they require a years payment up front. Intuit allows for monthly payments.

For free ecommerce on your web site, open up a Paypal account and get the HTML code for payment buttons for free. Then put those buttons on your web site.

How to Reach a Billion People for Free!

Step 1 zero cost internet marketing

Now that your web site is up and running you should register it with at least the top 3 search engines. 1. Google 2. Bing 3. Yahoo.

Step 2 zero cost internet marketing

Write and submit a **press release**. Google "free press release sites" for press release sites that will allow you to summit press releases for free. I you do not know how to write a press release go to www.fiverr.com and sub-contract the work out for only $5.00 !!!

Step 3 zero cost internet marketing

Write and submit articles to article marketing web sites like **ezinearticles.com.**

Step 4 zero cost internet marketing

Create and submit videos to video sharing sites like dailymotion.com or **youtube.com.** Make sure to include a hyperlink to your website in the description of your videos.

Step 5 zero cost internet marketing

Submit your web site to **dmoz.org**. This is a huge open directory that many smaller search engines go to get web sites for their database.

How to Reach a Billion People for Free!

YouTube has over a billion users. You may already have a YouTube channel and be good at making videos. However if you are not familiar with getting videos made and uploaded to YouTube you can go to a website called....

fiverr

https://www.fiverr.com/

https://goo.gl/R9x7NU

https://goo.gl/B7uF4L

https://goo.gl/YZ6VdS

https://goo.gl/RoPurV

At fiverr you can get a YouTube video created quickly and easily for only $5.00.
    (currently there is also a $1 service fee)

So for less than a movie ticket you can have a commercial for your real estate or business running 24 hours a day 7 days a week.

Once the video is uploaded you need to know how to get people to view your video. That's where SEO search engine optimization comes in.

How to Reach a Billion People for Free!

Getting Your Video Seen

YouTube reads any interaction that the viewer takes with your video as a sign that your video is interesting. So a Thumbs up or like will boost the ranking of your video.

Viewer comments can boost a video in the search rankings. So one tip for getting a viewer to leave a comment is to say "I'm curious what do you think about (insert topic). Another way to get viewer comments is to create a video about gun control laws, race relations, abortion rights or any other controversial topic.

YouTube can send a notice to all of your Subscribers every time you upload a video. So the more subscribers you have, the better chance that your video will get views, and views help the rank the video higher in the YouTube search results.

Getting your viewer to share a link to their social media pages is what makes our video go viral. Great or entertaining content is the key. It also does not hurt to simply ask the viewer to do it.

Rather than say the same thing every video, you can create a "close" video and upload it to YouTube. Then you can use the YouTube editor to add it to any video you upload.

How to Reach a Billion People for Free!

Search Engine Optimization (SEO) is the term used for the techniques used to drive traffic to your video. Many people use tactics that are against YouTube rules to drive traffic to their videos. These are call "Black Hat". There are plenty of web sites where you can purchase views to your videos. I would advise that you stay away from any possible unethical tactics. Get your views organically.

You can start your video off with good traffic, by sending it in a link to all the people you email to on a regular basis.

Google Keyword Tool

You begin your SEO by using the Google Keyword Tool. Go to

 https://adwords.google.com/KeywordPlanner

Once there you type in your root keyword or keyword phrase. Google will then give you about 700-1200 results that it thinks is relevant to your original keyword or phrase. Selecting the right keywords for your video is the key to being able to rank your videos.

You can get other keywords from the web site:

https://www.seocentro.com/

In the SEO tools box, select keyword suggestion.

How to Reach a Billion People for Free!

How to Select Your Keywords

Once you have your keyword results you can sort the results by relevance. This will give you a high chance for ranking for the original keyword or phrase that you entered.

You can sort your results by competition. You can chose low competition keywords or phrase to increase your chances of getting ranked. The low competition usually have less "per month" searches, but a combination of a few rankings can sometimes be better that just getting one keyword to rank.

Article Marketing

Ezine Articles is one of the top Article Marketing sites on the internet. You can join for free at http://ezinearticles.com/. Once you join the site you can upload articles to this web site that are relevant to your YouTube video. Ezine allows for you to place a link in your article. The link can go back to your YouTube traffic and dramatically increase the views.

When you write your article you should try to match as much as you can to your YouTube video. Use the same headlines, titles and description, as much as possible. YouTube and Google love relevance.

How to Reach a Billion People for Free!

Your article should be between 700 and 800 words. This is about the size that many blogs prefer. Once your article is uploaded onto Ezine articles, it can be picked up by any web site in the world. I once had an article about marketing photography get picked up by almost 800 blogs around the world. Many of them left the link placed in the article, and that allowed for tons of traffic to be drawn to my videos or web site. Not all blogs are ethical and many will remove your link, to keep traffic on their web site. Many will also replace you link with theirs. You won't know until you try.

Press Releases

One of the most powerful ways to increase traffic to your videos is to write and submit a press release. If you have never written a press release don't be intimidated. Your can go to a website www.fiverr.com and get a press release written for only $5.00!

If you want to write the press release yourself here are some tips.

The basic format is 3 paragraphs on one page, for immediate release. Unless it involves a date like a holiday in which you might want to have the editor delay the release.

How to Reach a Billion People for Free!

The headline should be attention getting. If you don't get the attention of the editor, the rest of the press release will not get read. Go to press release websites and look at press releases that have been published and study the headlines and the proper format.

After you have crafted your headline you write 3 paragraphs. The first paragraph is a short summary of what your story is all about. "But I have so much to tell I can't summarize it in a short paragraph." The revolutionary war has a ton of tremendous stories. Entire 2 hour movies have been made about it. Here is a two sentence description of those events. The future United States colonies fought the British. The colonies won!

Paragraph two is descriptions your story. Keep it in the form of a news story. Do not try to sell in your press release. Entertainment show are good at bringing on a celebrity, making small take, then ending the interview with a pitch or plug for their product or cause...

Paragraph three is your call to action. "For more information about how to help the victims of dipsy-doodle-itis call 555-1212 or hit this link."

Most press release website will allow you to place at least one link in your press release.

How to Reach a Billion People for Free!

Here is a list of the top five free press release websites:

Top Free Press Release Websites

https://www.prlog.org

https://www.pr.com

https://www.pr-inside.com

https://www.newswire.com

https://www.OnlinePRNews.com

How to Reach a Billion People for Free!

Social Media Websites

When you upload your videos to YouTube you should comment and like your own video. Once you like your own video, YouTube will give you the option to link the video to powerful social media websites. So you need to join these websites before you upload your videos. Below is a list of some of the social media websites you should join. When you link your videos to these websites, it creates a backlink to a highly rated website, which in turn factors into YouTube and Google's algorithm of what video is considered relevant and most popular.

Social Media Websites

https://www.facebook.com

https://www.tumbler.com

https://www.pinterest.com

https://www.reddit.com

https://www.linkedin.com/

http://digg.com/

https://twitter.com

https://plus.google.com/

How to Reach a Billion People for Free!

Finally, one of the most successful marketing methods being used today is "Permission Marketing". That is where you get a potential customer to give you their email address, and thus permission to market them.

You need a marketing automation platform and an email marketing service. These companies store and send out your emails.

Getresponse, MailChimp and Aweber are some of the more popular email storage autoresponder companies.

To build up and email list you usually have to offer a free product, report or book in exchange for the email address. Then you send them to a web page that captures and stores the email address. An example of my own email capture page is at the end of this book.

For detailed training videos on this and other marketing training type in the link below.

https://goo.gl/3bsRwg

Chapter 7

Business Insurance

BUSINESS INSURANCE

Consult an attorney for any and all of your business matters.

In the early 1990's an elderly woman purchased a hot cup of coffee from a McDonald's drive-thru window in Albuquerque. She spilled the coffee, and suffered 3rd degree burns. She sued Mcdonald's and won. She won 2.7 million dollars in a punitive damages victory. The verdict was appealed and settlement is estimated at somewhere in the neighborhood of $500,000 dollars. All because she spilled the coffee into her lap, while trying to add sugar and cream.

Two men in Ohio, were carpet layers. They were severely burned when a three and a half gallon container of carpet adhesive ignited, when the hot water heater it was sitting next to, was turned on. They felt the warning lable on the back of the can was insufficient. So they filed a lawsuit against the adhesive manufacturers and were awarded nine million dollars.

A woman in Oklahoma, purchased a brad new Winnebago. While driving it home, she set the cruise control to 70 miles per hour. She then left the drivers seat to make some coffee or a sandwich in the back of the motor home.

BUSINESS INSURANCE

The vehicle crashed and the woman sued Winnebago for not advising her, that cruise control does not drive and steer the vehicle. She won 1.7 million dollars and the company had to rewrite their instruction manual.

Unfortunately all three outrageous lawsuits are real. If you are going to run a business, any business, you should consider protecting yourself with Professional Liability Insurance, also known as Errors and Omissions (E & 0) insurance.

This type of insurance can help to protect you from having to pay the full cost of defending yourself against a negligence lawsuit claim.

Error and Omissions can protect you against claims that are not usually covered in regular liability insurance. Those policies usually cover bodily harm, or damage to property. Error and Omissions can protect you agaist negligence, and other mental anguish like inaccurate advice, or misrepresentation. Criminal prosecution is not covered.

Errors and Ommision insurance is recommended for notaries public, real estate brokers or investors and professionals like: software engineers, lawyers, home inspectors web site delvelopers and landscape architects to name a few professions.

BUSINESS INSURANCE

The Most Common Errors and Omission Claims:

%25 Breach of Fiduciary Duty

%15 Breach of Contract

%14 Negligence

%13 Failure to Supervise

%11 Unsuitability

%10 Other

BUSINESS INSURANCE

Things you should know about or require before purchasing a Errors and Omission policy is...

* What is the limit of liability

* What is the Deductible

* Does it include FDD First Dollar Defense - which obligates the insurance company to fight a case without a deductible first.

* Do I have Tail-end coverage or Extended Reporting Coverage (insurance that lasts into retirement)

* Extended coverage for Employees

* Cyber Liability Coverage

* Department of Labor Fiduciary Coverage

* Insolvency Coverage

If you get Errors and Omission insurance, renew it the day it expires. You must be careful to avoid gaps in your coverage, or it could result in not getting your policy renewed.

BUSINESS INSURANCE

A few E & O Insurance Providers:

Insureon

Insureon states that their median Errors and Omissions Insurance policy cost about $750 a year or about $65 a month. The price of course will vary according to your business, the policy you choose and other risk factors.

https://www.insureon.com/home

EOforless

EOforless.com helps insurance, investment, and real estate professionals buy E & O insurance at an affordable cost in five minutes or less.

https://www.eoforless.com/

BUSINESS INSURANCE

CalSurance Associates

As a leading insurance broker, CalSurance Associates, a division of Brown & Brown Program Insurance Services, Inc. has over fifty years of experience delivering comprehensive insurance products, exceptional service, and proven results to over 150,000 insured. They serve professionals nationwide and across multiple industries, including some of the largest financial firms and insurance companies in the United States.

http://www.calsurance.com/csweb/index.aspx

Better Safe Than Sorry

Insurance is one of the hidden costs of doing business. These are just a few companies and a brief overview on the topic of business insurance. Make sure to talk to an attorney or quailified insurance agent before making any decision on insurance. Protece you and your business. Many states do not require E & O insurances. But when you see the cost of some of the settlements, it's better to be safe than sorry.

Chapter 8

Business Terms

Business Terms & Definitions

Accounts – Companies produce a annual set of accounts. If you are listed on the stock exchange you have to give info on profits six months into the financial year.

Actuary – Actuaries work for insurance companies and pension providers and calculate life expectancy, accident rates and likely payouts by using math algorithms.

BARISTA - The person who prepares coffee at a coffee bar.

Business Plan – A business plan is a formal statement of business goals, reasons they are attainable, and plans for reaching them. It may also contain background information about the organization or team attempting to reach those goals.

Balance Sheet – a statement of the assets, liabilities, and capital of a business or other organization at a particular point in time, detailing, the balance of income and expenditure over the preceding period.

Business Terms & Definitions

Bear Market – A stock market in which share prices fall precipitously, typically 15%-20%.

Bull Market – A market when prices roar ahead.

CAPPUCCINO - An espresso shot combined with foamed steamed milk. Five to seven ounces total.

CHEMEX - The classic hourglass-shaped filter coffee brewer. Chemex filters are denser than other paper filters, and many believe that this creates a sweeter, well-balanced cup of coffee.

Capital Gains – A capital gain refers to profit that results from a sale of a capital asset, such as stock, bond or real estate, where the sale price exceeds the purchase price. The gain is the difference between a higher selling price and a lower purchase price.

Capital Gains Tax – a tax levied on profit from the sale of property or of an investment.

Business Terms & Definitions

Chapter 11 Bankruptcy – Chapter 11 is a chapter of Title 11 of the United States Bankruptcy Code, which permits reorganization under the bankruptcy laws of the United States. Chapter 11 bankruptcy is available to every business, whether organized as a corporation, partnership or sole proprietorship, and to individuals, although it is most prominently used by corporate entities.

Consumers Prices Index – The Consumer Price Index (CPI) is a measure that examines the weighted average of prices of a basket of consumer goods and services, such as transportation, food and medical care. It is calculated by taking price changes for each item in the predetermined basket of goods and averaging them.

Day Trading - Day Trading is the buying and selling of stocks during the trading day buy punters on their own account. The aim is to make a profit on the day and have no open positions at the close of the trading session.

Dow Jones Industrial Average – The Dow Jones Industrial Average (DJIA) is a price-weighted average of 30 significant stocks traded on the New York Stock Exchange (NYSE) and the NASDAQ. The DJIA was invented by Charles Dow back in 1896.

Business Terms & Definitions

Diminishing Returns – used to refer to a point at which the level of profits or benefits gained is less than the amount of money or energy invested.

Economic Growth – Economic growth is the increase in the inflation adjusted market value of the goods and services produced by an economy over time. It is conventionally measured as the percent rate of increase in real gross domestic product or real GDP.

Equity – the value of the shares issued by a company.

Elasticity – elasticity is a measure of a variable's sensitivity to a change in another variable. In business and economics, elasticity refers the degree to which individuals, consumers or producers change their demand or the amount supplied in response to price or income changes.

ESPRESSO - Concentrated coffee made when hot water is forced at pressure through fine coffee grounds. Usually slightly less than 2 ounces total. Baristas prefer 8 to 10 bars of pressure and 15 to 25 grams of coffee.

Business Terms & Definitions

Fiscal Year – The US fiscal year runs from October 1 to September 30.

FLAT WHITE - Espresso with flat, steamed milk, about 5 to 7 ounces.

FRENCH PRESS - Coffee made by steeping grounds with hot water in a vessel with a plunger and metal filter that pushes the grounds to the bottom. Often used in coffee bars for limited-edition coffees. Also called a press pot.

Foreign Exchange (Forex) – Foreign exchange, or forex, markets are where one currency is exchanged for another.

FORM 501 – A 501(c) organization is a nonprofit organization in the federal law of the United States according to 26 U.S.C. 501 and is one of 29 types of nonprofit organizations which are exempt from some federal income taxes.

Form 701 – General Information. Registration of a Limited Liability Partnership.

Business Terms & Definitions

GREEN BEANS - Unroasted coffee beans.

Grant – Grants are non-repayable funds or products disbursed or gifted by one party (grant makers), often a government department, corporation, foundation or trusts to a recipient, often (but not always) a nonprofit entity, educational institution, business or an individual.

Gross Domestic Product – GDP is the sum of all goods and services produced in the economy, including the service sector, manufacturing, construction, energy, agriculture and government.

Gross National Product – the total value of goods produced and services provided by a country during one year, equal to the gross domestic product plus the net income from foreign investments.

Hedge Funds – a limited partnership of investors that uses high risk methods, such as investing with borrowed money, in hopes of realizing large capital gains.

Income Statement – An income statement is one of the financial statements of a company and shows the company's revenues and expenses during a particular period.

Business Terms & Definitions

Income Tax – tax levied by a government directly on income, especially an annual tax on personal income.

Inheritance Tax – a tax imposed on someone who inherits property or money.

Inflation – a general increase in prices and fall in the purchasing value of money.

LATTE - Espresso with steamed milk, 8 ounces or more total.

Limited Liability Company (LLC) – A limited liability company (LLC) is a corporate structure whereby the members of the company cannot be held personally liable for the company's debts or liabilities. Limited liability companies are essentially hybrid entities that partnership or sole proprietorship.

Loan to Value – The loan-to-value (LTV) ratio is a financial term used by lenders to express the ratio of a loan to the value of an asset purchased. The term is commonly used by banks and building societies to represent the ration of the first mortgage line as a percentage of the total appraised value of real property.

Business Terms & Definitions

MACCHIATO - Espresso topped with a dab of foamed steamed milk, about 2 to 3 ounces total.

Microloan – a small sum of money lent at low interest to a new business.

MOCHA - Espresso mixed with chocolate syrup and steamed milk.

Mutual Fund – an investment program funded by shareholders that trades in diversified holdings and is professionally managed.

NASDAQ – The National Association of Securities Dealers Automated Quotations (NASDAQ) was set up in 1971 as an international screen-based trading system without a central dealing floor. In 1998 it merged with the American Stock exchange (Amex).

Occupational Pension Scheme – Occupational pension schemes may be contributory or non-contributory, funded or unfunded, defined benefit or defined contribution. In contributory schemes, both you and your employer pay contributions towards the scheme. In non-contributory schemes, you do not contribute buy your employer does.

Business Terms & Definitions

Partnership – A legal form of business operation between tow or more individuals who share management and profits. The federal government recognizes several types of partnerships. The two most common are general and limited partnerships. A limited partnership has both general and limited partners.

Rate of Return – A rate of return is the gain or loss on an investment over a specified time period, expressed as a percentage of the investment's cost. Gains on investments are defined as income received plus any capital gains realized on the sale of the investment.

Real Estate Investment Trusts – A real estate investment trust (REIT) is a company that owns, and in most cases operates, income-producing real estate. REITs own many types of commercial real estate, ranging from office and apartment buildings to warehouses, shopping centers and hotels.

REDEYE - A cup of brewed coffee with espresso.

RISTRETTO - Espresso pulled short — with less water — for a smaller, more concentrated drink.

Business Terms & Definitions

SBA - The Small Business Administration (SBA0 is a U.S. Government agency, formulated in 1953, that operates autonomously. This agency was established to bolster and promote the economy in general by providing assistance to small businesses.

SCORE (SBA) – SCORE is a nonprofit organization that provides free business mentoring services to prospective and established small business owners in the United States. More than 10,000 volunteers provide these services, with all volunteers being active and retired business executives and entrepreneurs.

Sole Proprietorship – A business that legally has no separate existence from its owner. Income and losses are taxed on the individual's personal income tax return. The sole proprietorship is the simplest business form under which one can operate a business. The sole proprietorship is not a legal entity.

Tax Haven – Generic term for geographical area outside the jurisdiction of one's home country which imposes only a few restriction on legitimate business activities within its jurisdiction, and little or no income tax. Also called a low tax jurisdiction, non tax jurisdiction, or offshore haven.

Business Terms & Definitions

Value Added Tax – A value added tax (VAT) is a consumption tax added to a product's sales price. It represents a tax on the "value added" to the product throughout its production process.

Wall Street – Wall Street is a street in lower Manhattan that is the original home of the New York Stock Exchange and the historic headquarters of the largest U.S. Brokerages and investment banks.

Yield – The yield is the income return on an investment, such as the interest or dividends received from holding a particular security. The yield is usually expressed as an annual percentage rate based on the investment's cost, current market value or face value.

Zero Interest Rates – A zero interest rate policy is a route taken by a central bank to keep the base rate at zero percent in an attempt to stimulate demand in the economy by making the supply of money cheaper.

Web Site

Coffee Shop

Business

Directory

Coffee Shop Supply Rolodex

ADT https://goo.gl/cRXmVv

https://www.appliancesconnection.com/

https://www.baristaproshop.com/

https://www.coffeeam.com/

https://www.coffeeshopsolutions.com/

https://www.danishpastryhous.com/wholesale-pastry/

https://www.discountmugs.com/

https://www.foodservicedirect.com/foods.html

https://www.espressoparts.com/

https://www.hotcupfactory.com/

Coffee Shop Supply Rolodex

https://www.markertek.com/

www.nationalbankcard.com

https://www.restaurantfurniture4less.com/

https://simplisafe.com/business-security

https://www.stickermule.com/

https://www.Walmart.com

https://www.webstaurantstore.com

https://www.wholelattelove.com/

$10,000 MegaSized Internet Marketing & Copy Writing & SEO Course & $1,000 Value Bonus

LIBRARY I (Video Training Programs)
1. Product Creation
2. Copy Writing & Payment
3. Auto Responder & Product Download Page
4. How to start a Freelancing business
5. Video Marketing
6. List Building
7. Affiliate Marketing
8. How to Get Massive Web Site Traffic

LIBRARY II (Video Training Programs)
1. Goldmine Government Grants
2. How to Write a Business Plan
3. Secrets to making money on eBay
4. Credit Repair
5. Goal Setting
6. Asset Protection How to Incorporate

$10,000 MegaSized Internet Marketing & Copy Writing & SEO Course & $1,000 Value Bonus

Library III
1. SEO SIMPLIFIED PART 1
2. SEO SIMPLIFIED PART 2
3. SEO Private Network Blogs
4. SEO Social Signals
5. SEO Profits

Bonus 1000 Package!
1. Insider Secrets to Government Contracts (PDF)
2. 1000 Books/Guides (text files)
3. Vacation Discounts (text file w/links to discounts)
4. Media Players (3 Software Programs)
100% MONEY BACK GUARANTEE!!!
ALL ON A 8 GIGABYTE FLASH DRIVE

This Massive Library with a $10,000 value all for only a
1 time payment of $67!!!
Get Instant Access by Using the Link Below:

https://urlzs.com/p7v3T

Leave a review and join Our VIP Mailing List Then Get All our Audio Books Free! We will be releasing over 100 money making audio books within the next 12 months! Just leave a review and join our mailing list and get them all for free!

Just Hit/Type in the Link Below

https://urlzs.com/HfbGF

www.ingramcontent.com/pod-product-compliance
Lightning Source LLC
Chambersburg PA
CBHW050331120526
44592CB00014B/2133